Tucholsky
Wagner
Zola
Scott
Sydow
Fonatne
Freud
Schlegel
Turgenev
Wallace
Twain
Walther von der Vogelweide
Fouqué
Friedrich II. von Preußen
Weber
Freiligrath
Frey
Fechner
Fichte
Weiße Rose
von Fallersleben
Kant
Ernst
Richthofen
Frommel
Engels
Fielding
Hölderlin
Eichendorff
Tacitus
Dumas
Fehrs
Faber
Flaubert
Feuerbach
Maximilian I. von Habsburg
Fock
Eliasberg
Eliot
Zweig
Ebner Eschenbach
Ewald
Vergil
Goethe
Elisabeth von Österreich
London
Mendelssohn
Balzac
Shakespeare
Dostojewski
Ganghofer
Trackl
Lichtenberg
Rathenau
Doyle
Gjellerup
Stevenson
Tolstoi
Hambruch
Droste-Hülshoff
Mommsen
Lenz
Thoma
Hanrieder
Dach
Verne
von Arnim
Hägele
Hauff
Humboldt
Reuter
Rousseau
Hagen
Hauptmann
Gautier
Karrillon
Garschin
Defoe
Hebbel
Baudelaire
Damaschke
Descartes
Hegel
Kussmaul
Herder
Wolfram von Eschenbach
Schopenhauer
Darwin
Dickens
Rilke
George
Bronner
Melville
Grimm Jerome
Bebel
Proust
Campe
Horváth
Aristoteles
Voltaire
Federer
Herodot
Bismarck
Vigny
Barlach
Heine
Gengenbach
Storm
Casanova
Tersteegen
Grillparzer
Georgy
Lessing
Gilm
Chamberlain
Langbein
Gryphius
Brentano
Lafontaine
Strachwitz
Claudius
Schiller
Kralik
Iffland
Sokrates
Katharina II. von Rußland
Bellamy
Schilling
Gerstäcker
Raabe
Gibbon
Tschechow
Löns
Hesse
Hoffmann
Gogol
Wilde
Vulpius
Luther
Heym
Hofmannsthal
Gleim
Roth
Klee
Hölty
Morgenstern
Goedicke
Heyse
Klopstock
Kleist
Luxemburg
Puschkin
Homer
Mörike
Machiavelli
La Roche
Horaz
Musil
Navarra
Aurel
Musset
Kierkegaard
Kraft
Kraus
Nestroy
Marie de France
Lamprecht
Kind
Kirchhoff
Hugo
Moltke
Nietzsche
Nansen
Laotse
Ipsen
Liebknecht
Marx
Ringelnatz
von Ossietzky
Lassalle
Gorki
Klett
Leibniz
May
vom Stein
Lawrence
Irving
Petalozzi
Platon
Knigge
Sachs
Pückler
Michelangelo
Kock
Kafka
Poe
Liebermann
de Sade
Praetorius
Mistral
Zetkin
Korolenko

The publishing house tredition has created the series **TREDITION CLASSICS**. It contains classical literature works from over two thousand years. Most of these titles have been out of print and off the bookstore shelves for decades.

The book series is intended to preserve the cultural legacy and to promote the timeless works of classical literature. As a reader of a **TREDITION CLASSICS** book, the reader supports the mission to save many of the amazing works of world literature from oblivion.

The symbol of **TREDITION CLASSICS** is Johannes Gutenberg (1400 – 1468), the inventor of movable type printing.

With the series, tredition intends to make thousands of international literature classics available in printed format again – worldwide.

All books are available at book retailers worldwide in paperback and in hardcover. For more information please visit: www.tredition.com

tredition was established in 2006 by Sandra Latusseck and Soenke Schulz. Based in Hamburg, Germany, tredition offers publishing solutions to authors and publishing houses, combined with worldwide distribution of printed and digital book content. tredition is uniquely positioned to enable authors and publishing houses to create books on their own terms and without conventional manufacturing risks.

For more information please visit: www.tredition.com

What the Schools Teach and Might Teach

John Franklin Bobbitt

Imprint

This book is part of the TREDITION CLASSICS series.

Author: John Franklin Bobbitt
Cover design: toepferschumann, Berlin (Germany)

Publisher: tredition GmbH, Hamburg (Germany)
ISBN: 978-3-8491-4874-4

www.tredition.com
www.tredition.de

Copyright:
The content of this book is sourced from the public domain.

The intention of the TREDITION CLASSICS series is to make world literature in the public domain available in printed format. Literary enthusiasts and organizations worldwide have scanned and digitally edited the original texts. tredition has subsequently formatted and redesigned the content into a modern reading layout. Therefore, we cannot guarantee the exact reproduction of the original format of a particular historic edition. Please also note that no modifications have been made to the spelling, therefore it may differ from the orthography used today.

WHAT THE SCHOOLS TEACH AND MIGHT TEACH

by

FRANKLIN BOBBITT
Assistant Professor of Educational Administration
The University of Chicago

1915

CLEVELAND EDUCATION SURVEY
Leonard P. Ayres, Director

The Survey Committee of the Cleveland Foundation
Cleveland, Ohio

Charles E. Adams, Chairman
Thomas G. Fitzsimons
Myrta L. Jones
Bascom Little
Victor W. Sincere

Arthur D. Baldwin, Secretary
James R. Garfield, Counsel
Newton D. Baker, Counsel
Alien T. Burns, Director

FOREWORD

This report on "What the Schools Teach and Might Teach" is one of the 25 sections of the report of the Education Survey of Cleveland conducted by the Survey Committee of the Cleveland Foundation in 1915. Twenty-three of these sections will be published as separate monographs. In addition there will be a larger volume giving a summary of the findings and recommendations relating to the regular work of the public schools, and a second similar volume giving the summary of those sections relating to industrial education. Copies of all these publications may be obtained from the Cleveland Foundation. They may also be obtained from the Division of Education of the Russell Sage Foundation, New York City. A complete list will be found in the back of this volume, together with prices.

TABLE OF CONTENTS

LIST OF TABLES

PREFATORY STATEMENT

For an understanding of some of the characteristics of this report it is necessary to mention certain of the conditions under which it was prepared.

The printed course of study for the elementary schools to be found in June, 1915, the time the facts were gathered for this report, was prepared under a former administration. While its main outlines were still held to, it was being departed from in individual schools in many respects. Except occasionally it was not possible to find record of such departures. It was believed that to accept the printed manual as representing current procedure would do frequent injustice to thoughtful, constructive workers within the system. But it must be remembered that courses of study for the city cover the work of twelve school years in a score and more of subjects, distributed through a hundred buildings. Only a small fraction of this comprehensive program is going on during any week of the school year; and of this fraction only a relatively small amount could actually be visited by one man in the time possible to devote to the task. In the absence of records of work done or of work projected, unduly large weight had to be given to the recommendations set down in the latest published course of study manual.

New courses of study were being planned for the elementary schools. This in itself indicated that the manual could not longer be regarded as an authoritative expression of the ideas of the administration. Yet with the exception of a good arithmetic course and certain excellent beginnings of a geography course, little indication could be found as to what the details of the new courses were to be. The present report has had to be written at a time when the administration by its acts was rejecting the courses of study laid out in the old manual, and yet before the new courses were formulated. Under the circumstances it was not a safe time for setting forth the *facts*, since not even the administration knew yet what the new courses were to be in their details. It was not a safe time to be either praising or blaming course of study requirements. The situation was too unformed for either. In the matter of the curriculum, the city was confessedly on the eve of a large constructive program. Its face was toward the future, and not toward the past; not even toward the present.

It was felt that if the brief space at the disposal of this report could also look chiefly toward the future, and present constructive recommendations concerning things that observation indicated should be kept in mind, it would accomplish its largest service. The time that the author spent in Cleveland was mostly used in observations in the schools, in consultation with teachers and supervisors, and in otherwise ascertaining what appeared to be the main outlines of practice in the various subjects. This was thought to be the point at which further constructive labors would necessarily begin.

The recommendation of a thing in this report does not indicate that it has hitherto been non-existent or unrecognized in the system. The intention rather is an economical use of the brief space at our disposal in calling attention to what appear to be certain fundamental principles of curriculum-making that seem nowadays more and more to be employed by judicious constructive workers.

The occasional pointing out of incomplete development of the work of the system is not to be regarded as criticism. Both school people and community should remember that since schools are to fit people for social conditions, and since these conditions are continually changing, the work of the schools must correspondingly change. Social growth is never complete; it is especially rapid in our generation. The work of education in preparing for these ever-new conditions can likewise never be complete, crystallized, perfected. It must grow and change as fast as social conditions make such changes necessary. To point out such further growth-needs is not criticism. The intention is to present the disinterested, detached view of the outsider who, although he knows indefinitely less than those within the system about the details of the work, can often get the perspective rather better just because his mind is not filled with the details.

THE POINT OF VIEW

There is an endless, and perhaps worldwide, controversy as to what constitutes the "essentials" of education; and as to the steps to be taken in the teaching of these essentials. The safe plan for constructive workers appears to be to avoid personal educational philosophies and to read all the essentials of education within the needs and processes of the community itself. Since we are using this social point of view in making curriculum suggestions for Cleveland, it seems desirable first to explain just what we mean. Some of the matters set down may appear so obvious as not to require expression. They need, however, to be presented again because of the frequency with which they are lost sight of in actual school practice.

Children and youth are expected as they grow up to take on by easy stages the characteristics of adulthood. At the end of the process it is expected that they will be able to do the things that adults do; to think as they think; to bear adult responsibilities; to be efficient in work; to be thoughtful public-spirited citizens; and the like. The individual who reaches this level of attainment is educated, even though he may never have attended school. The one who falls below this level is not truly educated, even though he may have had a surplus of schooling.

To bring one's nature to full maturity, as represented by the best of the adult community in which one grows up, is true education for life in that community. Anything less than this falls short of its purpose. Anything other than this is education misdirected.

In very early days, when community life was simple, practically all of one's education was obtained through participating in community activities, and without systematic teaching. From that day to this, however, the social world has been growing more complex. Adults have developed kinds of activities so complicated that youth cannot adequately enter into them and learn them without systematic teaching. At first these things were few; with the years they have grown very numerous.

One of the earliest of these too-complicated activities was written language—reading, writing, spelling. These matters became necessities to the adult world; but youth under ordinary circumstances could not participate in them as performed by adults sufficiently to master them. They had to be taught; and the school thereby came into existence. A second thing developed about the same time was the complicated number system used by adults. It was too difficult for youth to master through participation only. It too had to be taught, and it offered a second task for the schools. In the early schools this teaching of the so-called Three R's was all that was needed, because these were the only adult activities that had become so complicated as to require systematized teaching. Other things were still simple enough, so that young people could enter into them sufficiently for all necessary education.

As community vision widened and men's affairs came to extend far beyond the horizon, a need arose for knowledge of the outlying world. This knowledge could rarely be obtained sufficiently through travel and observation. There arose the new need for the systematic teaching of geography. What had hitherto not been a human necessity and therefore not an educational essential became both because of changed social conditions.

Looking at education from this social point of view it is easy to see that there was a time when no particular need existed for history, drawing, science, vocational studies, civics, etc., beyond what one could acquire by mingling with one's associates in the community. These were therefore not then essentials for education. It is just as easy to see that changed social conditions of the present make necessary for every one a fuller and more systematic range of ideas in each of these fields than one can pick up incidentally. These things have thereby become educational essentials. Whether a thing today is an educational "essential" or not seems to depend upon two things: whether it is a human necessity today; and whether it is so complex or inaccessible as to require systematic teaching. The number of "essentials" changes from generation to generation. Those today who proclaim the Three R's as the sole "essentials" appear to be calling from out the rather distant past. Many things have since become essential; and other things are being added year by year. The normal method of education in things not yet put into the schools, is participation in those things. One gets his ideas from watching others and then learns to do by doing. There is no reason to believe that as the school lends its help to some of the more difficult things, this normal plan of learning can be set aside and another substituted. Of course the schools must take in hand the difficult portions of the process. Where complicated knowledge is needed, the schools must teach that knowledge. Where drill is required, they must give the drill. But the knowledge and the drill should be given in their relation to the human activities in which they are used. As the school helps young people to take on the nature of adulthood, it will still do so by helping them to enter adequately into the activities of adulthood. Youth will learn to think, to judge, and to do, by thinking, judging, and doing. They will acquire a sense of responsibility by bearing responsibility. They will take on serious forms of thought by doing the serious things which require serious thought.

It cannot be urged that young people have a life of their own which is to be lived only for youth's sake and without reference to the adult world about them. As a matter of fact children and youth are a part of the total community of which the mature adults are the natural and responsible leaders. At an early age they begin to perform adult activities, to take on adult points of view, to bear adult responsibilities. Naturally it is done in ways appropriate to their natures. At first it is imitative play, constructive play, etc. —nature's method of bringing children to observe the serious world about them, and to gird themselves for entering into it. The next stage, if normal opportunities are provided, is playful participation in the activities of their elders. This changes gradually into serious participation as they grow older, becoming at the end of the process responsible adult action. It is not possible to determine the educational materials and processes at any stage of growth without looking at the same time to that entire world of which youth forms a part, and in which the nature and abilities of their elders point the goal of their training.

The social point of view herein expressed is sometimes characterized as being utilitarian. It may be so; but not in any narrow or undesirable sense. It demands that training be as wide as life itself. It looks to human activities of every type: religious activities; civic activities; the duties of one's calling; one's family duties; one's recreations; one's reading and meditation; and the rest of the things that are done by the complete man or woman.

READING AND LITERATURE

The amount of time given to reading in the elementary schools of Cleveland, and the average time in 50 other cities[A] are shown in the following table:

TABLE 1.—TIME GIVEN TO READING AND LITERATURE

	Hours per year		Per cent of grade time	
Grade	Cleveland	50 cities	Cleveland	50 cities
1	317	266	43	31
2	317	235	36	26
3	279	188	32	21
4	196	153	22	16
5	161	126	18	13
6	136	117	15	12
7	152	98	17	10
8	152	97	17	10
Total	1710	1280	25	17

During the course of his school life, each pupil who finishes the elementary grades in Cleveland receives 1710 hours of recitation and directed study in reading as against an average of 1280 hours in progressive cities in general. This is an excess of 430 hours, or 34 per cent. The annual cost of teaching reading being about $600,000, this represents an excess annual investment in this subject of some $150,000. Whether or not this excess investment in reading is justified depends, of course, upon the way the time is used. If the city is aiming only at the usual mastery of the mechanics of reading and the usual introductory acquaintance with simple works of literary art, it appears that Cleveland is using more time and labor than other cities consider needful. If, on the other hand, this city is using the excess time for widely diversified reading chosen for its content value in revealing the great fields of history, industry, applied science, manners and customs in other lands, travel, exploration, inventions, biography, etc., and in fixing life-long habits of intelligent reading, then it is possible that it is just this excess time that produces the largest educational returns upon the investment.

[Footnote A: Henry W. Holmes, "Time Distribution by Subjects and Grades in Representative Cities." In the Fourteenth Year Book of the National Society for the Study of Education, Part I, 1915. University of Chicago Press.]

It would seem, however, from a careful study of the actual work and an examination of the printed documents, that the chief purpose of teaching reading in this city is, to use the terminology of its latest manual, "easy expressive oral reading in rich, well-modulated tone." It is true that other aims are mentioned, such as enlargement of vocabulary, word-study, understanding of expressions and allusions, acquaintance with the leading authors, appreciation of "beautiful expressions," etc. Properly emphasized, each of these purposes is valid; but there are other equally valid ends to be achieved through proper choice of the reading-content that are not mentioned. There is here no criticism of the purposes long accepted, but of the apparent failure to recognize other equally important ones. The character of the reading-content is referred to only in the recommendation that in certain grades it should relate to the seasons and to special occasions. Even in reference to the supplementary reading, where content should be the first concern, the only statement of purpose is that "children should read for the joy of it." Unfortunately, this mistaken emphasis is not at all uncommon among the schools of the nation. How one reads has received an undue amount of attention; what one reads in the school courses must and will receive an increasingly large share of time and thought, in the new evaluation. The use of interesting and valuable books for other educational purposes at the same time that they are used for drill in the mechanics of reading is coming more and more to be recognized as an improved mode of procedure. The mechanical side of reading is not thereby neglected. It is given its proper function and relation, and can therefore be better taught.

So far as one can see, Cleveland is attempting in the reading work little more than the traditional thing. The thirty-four per cent excess time may be justified by the city on the theory that the schools are commissioned to get the work done one-third better than in the average city. The reading tests made by the Survey fail to reveal any such superiority. The city appears to be getting no better than average results.

Certainly people should read well and effectively in all ways in which they will be called upon to read in their adult affairs. For the most part this means reading for ideas, suggestions, and information in connection with the things involved in their several callings; in connection with their civic problems; for recreation; and for such general social enlightenment as comes from newspapers, magazines, and books. Most reading will be for the content. It is desirable that the reading be easy and rapid, and that one gather in all the ideas as one reads. Because of the fact that oral reading is slower, more laborious for both reader and listener, and because of the present easy accessibility of printed matter, oral reading is becoming of steadily diminishing importance to adults. No longer should the central educational purpose be the development of expressive oral reading. It should be rapid and effective silent reading for the sake of the thought read.

To train an adult generation to read for the thought, schools must give children full practice in reading for the thought in the ways in which later as adults they should read. After the primary teachers have taught the elements, the work should be mainly voluminous reading for the sake of entering into as much of the world's thought and experience as possible. The work ought to be rather more extensive than intensive. The chief end should be the development of that wide social vision and understanding which is so much needed in this complicated cosmopolitan age. While works of literary art should constitute a considerable portion of the reading program, they should not monopolize the program, nor indeed should they be regarded as the most important part of it. It is history, travel, current news, biography, advance in the world of industry and applied science, discussions of social relations, political adjustments, etc., which adults need mostly to read; and it is by the reading of these things that children form desirable and valuable reading habits.

The reading curriculum needs to be looked after in two important ways. First, social standards of judgment should determine the nature of the reading. The texts beyond the primary grades are now for the most part selections of literary art. Very little of it has any conscious relation, immediate or remote, to present-day problems and conditions or with their historical background. Probably children should read many more selections of literary art than are found in the textbooks and the supplementary sets now owned by the schools. But certainly such cultural literary experience ought not to crowd out kinds of reading that are of much greater practical value. Illumination of the things of serious importance in the everyday world of human affairs should have a large place in reading work of every school.

It is true that the supplementary sets of books have been chosen chiefly for their content value. Many are historical, biographical, geographical, scientific, civic, etc., in character. On the side of content, they have advanced much farther than the textbooks toward what should constitute a proper reading course. Unfortunately, the schools are very incompletely supplied with these sets. If we consider all the sets of supplementary readers found in 10 or more schools, we find that few of those assigned for fourth-grade reading are found in one-quarter of the buildings and none are in half of them. The same is true of the books for use in the fifth and seventh grades. Some of the books for the sixth and eighth grades are found in more than half of the buildings, but there is none that is found in as many as three-quarters of them.

The second thing greatly needed to improve the reading course is more reading practice. One learns to do a thing easily, rapidly, and effectively by practice. The course of study in reading should therefore provide the opportunity for much practice. At present the reading texts used aggregate for the eight grades some 2100 pages. A third-grade child ought to read matter suitable for its intelligence at

20 pages per hour, and a grammar-grade child at 30 to 40 pages per hour. Since rapidity of reading is one of the desired ends, the practice reading should be rapid. At the moderate rates mentioned, the entire series of reading texts ought to be read in some 80 hours. This is 10 hours' practice for each of the eight school years, an altogether insufficient amount of rapid reading practice. Of course the texts can be read twice, or let us say three times, aggregating 30 hours of practice per year. But even this is not more than could easily be accomplished in two or three weeks of each of the years—always presuming that the reading materials are rightly adapted to the mental maturity of the pupils. This leaves 35 weeks of the year unprovided for. To make good this deficit, the buildings are furnished with supplementary books in sets sufficiently large to supply entire classes. The average number of such sets per building is shown in the following table:

TABLE 2.—SETS OF SUPPLEMENTARY READING BOOKS PER BUILDING

Grade Average number of sets 1 10.0 2 6.3 3 5.1 4 5.5 5 6.3 6 5.3 7 5.5 8 6.0

A fifth, sixth, seventh, or eighth-grade student ought to be able to read all the materials supplied his grade, both reading texts and all kinds of supplementary reading, in 40 or 50 hours. He ought to do it easily in six weeks' work, without encroaching on recitation time. He can read all of it twice in 10 weeks; and three times in 14 weeks. After reading everything three times over, there still remain 24 weeks of each year unprovided for.

The reply of teachers is that the work is so difficult that it has to be slowed down enough to consume these 24 weeks. But is not this to admit that the hill is too steep, that there is too much dead pull, and that the materials are ill-chosen for practice in habits of rapid intelligent reading? It is not by going slow that one learns to go fast. Quite the reverse. Too often the school runs on low speed gear when it ought to be running on high. The low may be necessary for the starting, but not for the running. It may be necessary in the primary grades, but not thereafter for those who have had a normal start. Reading practice should certainly make for increased speed in effective reading.

The actual work in the grades is very different from the plan suggested. In taking up any selection for reading, the plan in most schools is about as follows:

1. A list of the unusual words met with is written on the blackboard.

2. Teacher and pupils discuss the meaning of these words; but unfortunately words out of the context often carry no meaning.

3. The words are marked diacritically, and pronounced.

4. Pupils "use the words in sentences." The pupil frequently has nothing to say that involves the word. It is only given an imitation of a real use by being put into an artificial sentence.

5. The oral reading is begun. One pupil reads a paragraph.

6. With the book removed, the meaning of the paragraph is then reproduced either by the reader or some other pupil. This work is necessarily perfunctory because the pupil knows he is not giving information to anybody. Everybody within hearing already has the meaning fresh in mind from the previous reading. The normal child cannot work up enthusiasm for oral reproduction under such conditions.

7. The paragraph is analyzed into its various elements, and these in turn are discussed in detail.

Such work is not reading. It is analysis. A selection is not read, it is analyzed. The purpose of real reading is to enter into the thought and emotional experience of the writer; not to study the methods by which the author expressed himself. The net result when the work is done as described is to develop a critical consciousness of methods, without helping the children to enter normally and rightly into the experience of the writer. The children of Cleveland need this genuine training in reading.

Reading in the high schools needs very much the same sort of modernization. There are more kinds of literature than classical belles-lettres, and perhaps more important kinds. We would not advocate a reduction of the amount of aesthetic literature. Indeed, the young people of Cleveland need to enter into a far wider range of such literature than is the case at present. But the reading courses in high schools should be built out in ways already recommended for elementary schools.

The training, however, should be mainly in reading and not in analysis. The former is of surpassing importance to all people; the latter is important only to certain specialists. And, what is more, fullness of reading and right ways of reading will accomplish incidentally most of the things aimed at in the analysis.

The following table of the reading outline of the High School of Commerce is a fair sample of what the city is doing. Note how much time is given to the reading and analysis of the few selections covered in four years.

TABLE 3.—WEEKS GIVEN TO READING OF DIFFERENT BOOKS IN HIGH SCHOOL OF COMMERCE

Weeks to read

First Year
  Ashmun's Prose Selections 9
  Cricket on the Hearth 5
  Sohrab and Rustum 3
  Midsummer Night's Dream 6
  Ivanhoe 11

Second Year
  Autobiography of Franklin 7
  Idylls of the King 10
  Treasure Island 7
  Sketch Book 7
  Vision of Sir Launfal 3

Third Year
  Silas Marner 7
  Iliad (Bryant's—4 books) 5
  Washington's Farewell Address 5
  First Bunker Hill Oration 6
  Emerson's Compensation 5
  Roosevelt Book 6

Fourth Year
  Markham's The Man with the Hoe 2
  Tale of Two Cities 10
  Public Duty of the Educated Man 4
  Macbeth 11
  Self-Reliance 6

When a short play of a hundred pages like Macbeth requires nearly three months for reading, when almost two months are given to Treasure Island and nearly three months to Ivanhoe, clearly it is something other than reading that is being attempted. It is perfectly obvious that the high schools are attending principally to the mechanics of expression and not to the content of the expression. The relative emphasis should be reversed.

The amount of reading in the high schools should be greatly increased. Those who object that rapid work is superficial believe that work must be slow to be thorough. It should be remembered, however, that slow work is often superficial and that rapid work is often excellent. In fact the world's best workers are generally rapid, accurate, and thorough. Ask any business man of wide experience. Now leaving aside pupils who are slow by nature, it can be affirmed that pupils will acquire slow, thorough habits or rapid, thorough habits according to the way they are taught. If they are brought up by the slow plan, naturally when speeded up suddenly, the quality of their work declines. They can be rapid, accurate, and thorough only if such strenuous work begins early and is continued consistently. Slow habits are undesirable if better ones can just as well be implanted.

To avoid possible misunderstanding, it ought to be stated that the plan recommended does not mean less drill upon the mechanical side of reading. We are recommending a somewhat more modernized kind of mechanics, and a much more strenuous kind of drill. The plan looks both toward more reading and improved habits of reading.

One final suggestion finds here its logical place. Before the reading work of elementary or high schools can be modernized, the city must purchase the books used in the work. Leaving the supplying of books to private purchase is the largest single obstacle in the way of progress. Men in the business world will have no difficulty in seeing the logic of this. When shoes, for example, were made by hand, each workman could easily supply his own tools; but now that elaborate machinery has been devised for their manufacture, it has become so expensive that a machine factory must supply the tools. It is so in almost every field of labor where efficiency has been introduced. Now the books to be read are the tools in the teaching of reading. In a former day when a mastery of the mechanics of reading was all that seemed to be needed, the privately purchased textbook could suffice. In our day when other ends are set up beyond and above those of former days, a far more elaborate and expensive equipment is required. The city must now supply the educational tools. It is well to face this issue candidly and to state the facts plainly. Relative failure can be the only possible lot of reluctant communities. They can count on it with the same assurance as that of a manufacturer of shoes who attempts to employ the methods of former days in competition with modern methods.

In this city the expenditures for supplementary textbooks have amounted to something more than $31,000 in the past 10 years. Approximately one-third of this sum was spent in the first seven years of the decade and more than $20,000 in the past three years. This indicates the rapid advance in this direction made under the present school administration but the supply of books still falls far short of the needs of the schools. A fair start has been made but nothing should be permitted to obstruct rapid progress in this direction.

SPELLING

Cleveland has set apart an average amount of program time for spelling. Possibly the study might more accurately be called word-study, since it aims also at training for pronunciation, syllabification, vocabulary extension, and etymology. Since much of the reading time is given to similar word-study, the figures presented in Table 4 are really too small to represent actual practice in Cleveland.

TABLE 4.—TIME GIVEN TO SPELLING

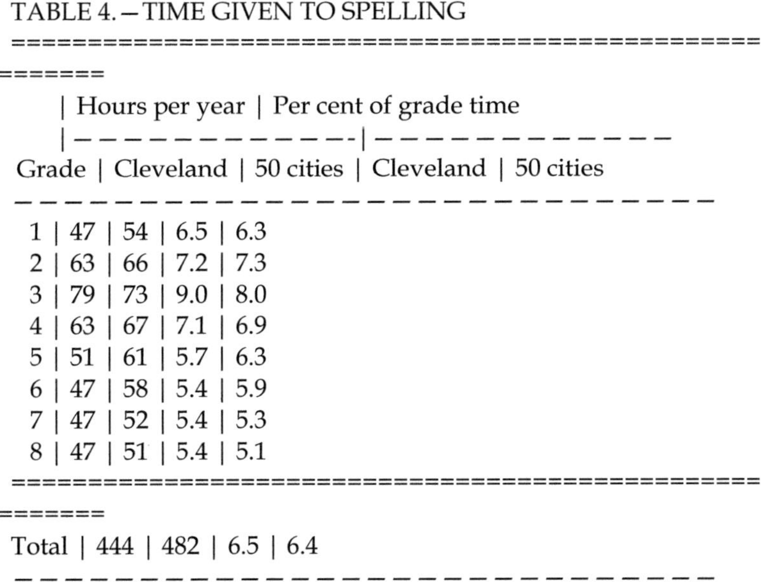

Grade	Hours per year — Cleveland	Hours per year — 50 cities	Per cent of grade time — Cleveland	Per cent of grade time — 50 cities
1	47	54	6.5	6.3
2	63	66	7.2	7.3
3	79	73	9.0	8.0
4	63	67	7.1	6.9
5	51	61	5.7	6.3
6	47	58	5.4	5.9
7	47	52	5.4	5.3
8	47	51	5.4	5.1
Total	444	482	6.5	6.4

The general plan of the course is indicated in the syllabus:

"Two words are made prominent in each lesson. Their pronunciation, division into syllables, derivation, phonetic properties, oral and written spelling and meaning, are all to be made clear to pupils.

"The teaching of a new word may be done by using it in a sentence; by definition or description; by giving a synonym or the antonym; by illustration with object, action or drawing; and by etymology.

"Each lesson should have also from eight to 20 subordinate words taken from textbook or composition exercises…. Frequent supplementary dictation, word-building and phonic exercises should be given. Spell much orally…. Teach a little daily, test thoroughly, drill intensively, and follow up words misspelled persistently."

In most respects the work agrees with the usual practice in progressive cities: the teaching of a few words in each lesson; the frequent and continuous review of words already taught; taking the words to be taught from the language experience of the pupils; following up words actually misspelled; studying the words from many angles, etc.

In some respects the work needs further modernization. The words chosen for the work are not always the ones most needed. Whether children or adults, people need to spell only when they write. They need to spell correctly the words of their writing vocabulary, and they need to spell no others. More important still, they need to acquire the habit of watching their spelling as they write; the habit of spelling every word with certainty that it is correct, and the habit of going to word-lists or dictionary when there is any doubt.

This development of the habit of watchfulness over their spelling as they write is the principal thing. One who has it will always spell well. In case he has much writing to do, it automatically leads to a constant renewing of his memory for words used and prevents forgetting. The one who has only memorized word-lists, even though they have been rigorously drilled, inevitably forgets, whether rapidly or slowly; and in proportion as he lacks this general habit of watchfulness, degenerates in his spelling. The reason why schools fail to overcome the frequent criticism that young people do not spell well, is because of the fact that they have been trying to teach specific words rather than to develop a general and constant watchfulness.

The fundamental training in spelling is accomplished in connection with composition, letter-writing, etc. Direct word-list study should have only a secondary and supplemental place. It is needed, first, for making people conscious of the letter elements of words which are seen as wholes in their reading, and for bringing them to look closely into the relations of these letter elements; second, for developing a preliminary understanding of the spelling of words used; and third, for drill upon words commonly misspelled. While a necessary portion of the entire process, it probably should not require so much time as is now given to it and the time saved should be devoted to the major task of teaching spelling watchfulness in connection with writing letters and compositions.

The great majority of the population of Cleveland will spell only as they write letters, receipts, and simple memoranda. They do not need to spell a wide vocabulary with complete accuracy. On the other hand, there are classes of people to whom a high degree of spelling accuracy covering a fairly wide vocabulary is an indispensable vocational necessity: clerks, copyists, stenographers, correspondents, compositors, proof-readers, etc. These people need an intensive specialized training in spelling that is not needed by the mass of the population. Such specialized vocational training should be taken care of by the Cleveland schools, but it should not be forced upon all simply because the few need it. The attempt to bring all to the high level needed by the few, and the failure to reach this level, is responsible for the justifiable criticism of the schools that those few who need to spell unusually well are imperfectly trained.

The spelling practice should continue through the high school. It is only necessary for teachers to refuse to accept written work that contains any misspelled word to force upon students the habit of watchfulness over every word written. The High School of Commerce is to be commended for making spelling a required portion of the training. The course needs to be more closely knit with composition and business letter-writing.

HANDWRITING

Cleveland gives a considerably larger proportion of time to handwriting than the average of the 50 cities.

TABLE 5.—TIME GIVEN TO HANDWRITING

Grade	Hours per year		Per cent of grade time	
	Cleveland	50 cities	Cleveland	50 cities
1	47	50	6.5	6.7
2	63	60	7.2	6.7
3	63	52	7.2	5.7
4	63	53	7.2	5.5
5	67	50	6.4	5.1
6	47	47	5.4	4.8
7	47	39	5.4	3.9
8	32	37	3.6	3.7
Total	419	388	6.1	5.1

The curriculum of handwriting resolves itself mainly into questions of method, and of standards to be achieved in each of the grades. These matters are treated intensively in the section of the survey report entitled "Measuring the Work of the Public Schools."

LANGUAGE, COMPOSITION, GRAMMAR

The schools devote about the usual amount of time to training for the correct use of the mother tongue. Most of the time in intermediate and grammar grades is devoted to English grammar. Composition receives only minor attention.

TABLE 6.—TIME GIVEN TO LANGUAGE, COMPOSITION, AND GRAMMAR

	Hours per year		Per cent of grade time	
Grade	Cleveland	50 cities	Cleveland	50 cities
1	79	75	10.9	8.6
2	95	79	10.8	8.7
3	79	94	9.0	10.3
4	104	106	11.8	10.9
5	120	116	13.6	12.0
6	120	118	13.6	12.2
7	125	134	14.3	13.7
8	125	142	14.3	14.1
Total	847	864	12.3	11.4

In the teaching of grammar too much stress is placed on forms and relations. Of course it is expected that this knowledge will be of service to the pupils in their everyday expression. But such practical application of the knowledge is not the thing toward which the work actually looks. The end really achieved is rather the ability to recite well on textbook grammar, and to pass good examinations in the subject. In classes visited the thing attempted was being done in a relatively effective way. And when judged in the light of the kind of education considered best 20 years ago, the work is of a superior character.

As a matter of fact, facility in oral and written expression is, like everything else, mainly developed through much practice. The form and style of expression are perfected mainly through the conscious and unconscious imitation of good models. Technical grammar plays, or should play, the relatively minor role of assisting students to eliminate and to avoid certain types of error. Since grammar has this perfectly practical function to perform, probably only those things needed should be taught; but more important still, every-thing taught should be constantly put to use by the pupils in their oversight of their own speech and writing. Only as knowledge is put to work, is it really learned or assimilated. The schools should require much oral and written expression of the pupils, and should enforce constant watchfulness of their own speech on the part of the pupils. It is possible to require pupils to go over all of their written work and to examine it, before handing it in, in the light of all the grammatical rules they have learned. It is also possible for pupils to guard consciously against known types of error which they are accustomed to make in their oral recitations. Every recitation in whatever subject provides opportunity for such training in habits of watchfulness. Only as the pupil is brought to do it himself, without prompting on the part of the teacher, is his education accomplished.

A limited amount of systematic grammatical teaching is a neces-sary preliminary step. The purpose is an introductory acquaintance with certain basic forms, terminology, relationships, and grammati-cal perspective. This should be accomplished rapidly. Like the pre-liminary survey in any field, this stage of the work will be relatively superficial. Fullness and depth of understanding will come with application. This preliminary understanding can not be learned "incidentally." Such a plan fails on the side of perspective and rela-tionship, which are precisely the things in which the preparatory teaching of the subject should be strong.

This preliminary training in technical grammar need not be either so extensive or so intensive as it is at present. An altogether dispro-portionate amount of time is now given to it. The time saved ought to go to oral and written expression,—composition, we might call it, except that the word has been spoiled because of the artificiality of the exercises.

The composition or expression most to be recommended consists of reports on the supplementary reading in connection with history, geography, industrial studies, civics, sanitation, etc.; and reports of observations on related matters in the community. Topics of interest and of value are practically numberless. Such reports will usually be oral; but often they will be written. Expression occurs naturally and normally only where there is something to be discussed. The present manual suggests compositions based upon "changes in trees, dissemination of seeds, migration of birds, snow, ice, clouds, trees, leaves, and flowers." This type of composition program under present conditions cannot be a vital one. Elementary science is not taught in the schools of Cleveland; and so the subject matter of these topics is not developed. Further, it is the world of human action, revealed in history, geography, travels, accounts of industry, commerce, manufacture, transportation, etc., that possesses the greater value for the purposes of education, as well as far greater interest for the student.

Probably little time should be set apart on the program for composition. The expression side of all the school work, both in the elementary school and in the high school, should be used to give the necessary practice. The technical matters needed can be taught in occasional periods set aside for that specific purpose.

The isolation of the composition work continues through the academic high schools and in considerable degree through the technical high schools also. In the high schools the expression work probably needs to be developed chiefly in the classes in science, history, industrial studies, commercial and industrial geography, physics, etc., where the students have an abundance of things to discuss. Probably four-fifths of all of the training in English expression in the high schools should be accomplished in connection with the oral and written work of the other subjects.

MATHEMATICS

To arithmetic, the Cleveland schools are devoting a somewhat larger proportion of time than the average of cities.

TABLE 7. — TIME GIVEN TO ARITHMETIC

Grade	Hours per year		Per cent of grade time	
	Cleveland	50 cities	Cleveland	50 cities
1	38	60	5.2	6.9
2	136	96	15.5	10.7
3	142	131	16.3	14.4
4	152	149	17.2	15.4
5	142	144	17.1	14.9
6	155	146	17.5	15.0
7	142	140	16.1	14.4
8	158	142	17.9	14.1
Total	1065	1008	15.5	13.3

That everybody should be well grounded in the fundamental operations of arithmetic is so obvious as to require no discussion. Beyond this point, however, difficult problems arise. The probabilities are that the social and vocational conditions of the coming generation will require that everybody be more mathematical-minded than at present.

The content of mathematics courses is to be determined by human needs. One of the fundamental needs of the age upon which we are now entering is accurate quantitative thinking in the fields of one's vocation, in the supervision of our many co-operative governmental labors, in our economic thinking with reference to taxation, expenditures, insurance, public utilities, civic improvements, pensions, corporations, and the multitude of other civic and vocational matters.

Just as the thought involved in physics, astronomy, or engineering needs to be put in mathematical terms in order that it may be used effectively, so must it be with effective vocational, civic, and economic thinking in general. Our chief need is not so much the ability to do calculations as it is the ability to think in figures and the habit of thinking in figures. Calculations, while indispensable, are incidental to more important matters.

Naturally before one is prepared to use mathematical forms of thought in considering the many social and vocational problems, he must have mastered the fundamentals. The elementary school, at as early an age as practicable, should certainly give the necessary preliminary knowledge of and practice in the fundamental operations of arithmetic. This should be done with a high degree of thoroughness, but it should always be kept in mind that this is only a preliminary mastery of the alphabet of mathematical thinking. The other part of our problem is a development of the quantitative aspects of the vocational, economic, and civic subjects. One finds clear recognition of this in Cleveland in the new arithmetic manual. The following quotations are typical:

"The important problem of the seventh and eighth grades is to enable the pupils to understand and deal intelligently with the most important social institutions with which arithmetical processes are associated."

In discussing the teaching of the mathematical aspect of insurance, we find this statement: "Owing to the important place this subject holds in life, we should emphasize its informational value rather than its mathematical content."

Under taxation and revenue: "If the general features of this subject are presented from the standpoint of civics, the pupils should have no difficulty in solving the problems as no new principle is introduced."

Under stocks and bonds: "Pupils should be taught to know what a corporation is, its chief officers, how it is organized, what stocks and bonds are, and how dividends are declared and paid, in so far as such knowledge is needed by the general public."

These statements indicate a recognition of the most important principle that should control in the development of all of the mathematics, elementary and secondary, beyond the preliminary training needed for accuracy and rapidity in the fundamental operations.

When this principle is carried through to its logical conclusion, it will be observed that most of these developments will not take place within the arithmetic class, but in the various other subjects. Arithmetic teaching, like the teaching of penmanship, etc., is for the purpose of giving tools that are to be used in matters that lie beyond. The full development will take place within these various other fields. For the present, it probably will be well for the schools to develop the matters both within the arithmetic classes and in the other classes. Neither being complete at present, each will tend to complete the other.

On the side of the preliminary training in the fundamental operations, the present arithmetic course of study is on the whole of a superior character. It provides for much drill, and for a great variety of drill. It emphasizes rapidity, accuracy, and the confidence that comes to pupils from checking up their results. It holds fast to fundamentals, dispensing with most of the things of little practical use. It provides easy advances from the simple to the complicated. The field of number is explored in a great variety of directions so that pupils are made to feel at home in the subject. One large defect is the lack of printed exercise materials, the use of which would result in greatly increased effectiveness. Such printed materials ought to be furnished in great abundance.

ALGEBRA

In the report of the Educational Commission of Cleveland, 1906, we find the following very significant sentences relative to the course of study for the proposed high school of commerce:

"An entirely new course of study should be made out for this school. Subjects which have been considered necessary in a high school, because they tend to develop the mind, should not for this reason only be placed in a commercial course. Subjects should not be given because they strengthen the mind, but the subjects which are necessary in this course should be given in such a way as to strengthen the mind. The mathematics in this school should consist of business arithmetic and mensuration. We can see no reason for giving these students either algebra or geometry. But they should be taught short and practical methods of working business problems."

We find here a recommendation since carried out that indicates a clear recognition of the principle of adaptation of the course of study to actual needs. Carried out to its logical conclusion, and applied to the entire city system, it raises questions as to the advisability of requiring algebra of girls in any of the high school courses; or of requiring it of that large number of boys looking forward to vocations that do not involve the generalized mathematics of algebra. Now either the commercial students do need algebra or a large proportion of these others do not need it. It seems advisable here to do nothing more than to present the question as one which the city needs to investigate. The present practice, in Cleveland as elsewhere, reveals inconsistency. In one or the other of the schools a wrong course is probably being followed. The current tendency in public education is toward agreement with the principle enunciated by the Cleveland Educational Commission, and toward a growing and consistent application of it.

Differentiation in the mathematics of different classes of pupils is necessary. The public schools ought to give the same mathematics to all up to that level where the need is common to all. Beyond that point, mathematics needs to be adapted to the probable future activities of the individual. There are those who will need to reach the higher levels of mathematical ability. Others will have no such need.

There is a growing belief that even for those who are in need of algebra the subject is not at present organized in desirable ways. It is thought that, on the one hand, it should be knit up in far larger measure with practical matters, and on the other, it should be developed in connection with geometry and trigonometry. The technical high schools of Cleveland have adopted this form of organization. Their mathematics is probably greatly in advance of that of the academic schools.

GEOMETRY

Form study should begin in the kindergarten, and it should develop through the grades and high school in ways similar to the arithmetic, and in conjunction with the arithmetic, drawing, and construction work. Since geometrical forms involve numerical relations, they supply good materials to use in making number relations concrete and clear. This is now done in developing ideas of fractions, multiplication, division, ratio, per cent, etc. It should be done much more fully and variously than at present and for the double purpose of practising the form-ideas as well as the number-ideas. Arithmetic study and form-study can well grow up together, gradually merging into the combined algebra and geometry so far as students need to reach the higher levels of mathematical generalization.

At the same time that this is being developed in the mathematics classes, development should also be going on in the classes of drawing, design, and construction. The alphabet of form-study will thus be taught in several of the studies. The application will be made in practical design, in mechanical and free-hand drawing, in constructive labor, in the graphical representation of social, economic, and other facts of life. The application comes not so much in the development of practical problems in the mathematics classes as in the development of the form aspect of those other activities that involve form.

We have here pointed to what appears to be in progressive schools a growing program of work. Everywhere it is yet somewhat vague and inchoate. In connection with the arithmetic, the drawing, the construction and art work, and the mathematics of the technical high schools, it appears to be developing in Cleveland in a vigorous and healthy manner.

HISTORY

The curriculum makers for elementary education do not seem to have placed a high valuation upon history. Apparently it has not been considered an essential study of high worth, like reading, writing, spelling, grammar, and arithmetic. To history are allotted but 290 hours in Cleveland, as against 496 hours in the average of 50 progressive American cities. This discrepancy should give the city pause and concern. If a mistake is being made, it is more likely to be on the part of an individual city than upon that of 50 cities. The probability is that Cleveland is giving too little time to this subject.

TABLE 8.—TIME GIVEN TO HISTORY

Grade	Hours per year		Per cent of grade time	
	Cleveland	50 cities	Cleveland	50 cities
1	0	27	0.0	3.1
2	0	31	0.0	3.4
3	19	35	2.1	3.8
4	25	57	2.9	5.8
5	25	67	2.9	6.9
6	51	71	5.7	7.3
7	85	91	9.7	9.2
8	85	117	9.7	11.6
Total	290	496	4.2	6.5

The treatment in the course of study manual indicates that it is a neglected subject. Of the 108 pages, it receives an aggregate of less than two. The perfunctory assignment of work for the seventh grade is typical:

"UNITED STATES HISTORY

"B Assignment.
Mace's History, pp. 1-124 inclusive.
Questions and suggested collateral reading
found in Appendix may be used as teacher directs.

"A Assignment.
Mace's History, pp. 125-197.
Make use of questions and suggested collateral
reading at your own option."

For fifth and sixth grades there is assigned a small history text of 200 pages for one or two lessons per week. The two years of the seventh and eighth grades are devoted to the mastery of about 500 pages of text. While there is incidental reference to collateral reading, as a matter of fact the schools are not supplied with the necessary materials for this collateral reading in the grammar grades. The true character of the work is really indicated by the last sentence of the eighth-grade history assignment: "The text of our book should be thoroughly mastered."

In discussing the situation, the first thing to which we must call attention is the great value of history for an understanding of the multitude of complicated social problems met with by all people in a democracy. In a country where all people are the rulers, all need a good understanding of the social, political, economic, industrial, and other problems with which we are continually confronted. It is true the thing needed is an understanding of present conditions, but there is no better key to a right understanding of our present conditions than history furnishes. One comes to understand a present situation by observing how it has come to be. History is one of the most important methods of social analysis.

The history should be so taught that it will have a demonstrably practical purpose. In drawing up courses of study in the subject for the grammar grades and the high school, the first task should be an

46

analysis of present-day social conditions, the proper understanding of which requires historical background. Once having discovered the list of social topics, it is possible to find historical readings which will show how present conditions have grown up out of earlier ones. Looked at from a practical point of view, the history should be developed on the basis of topics, a great abundance of reading being provided for each of the topics. We have in mind such topics as the following:

Sociological Aspects of War
Territorial Expansion
Race Problems
Tariff and Free Trade
Transportation
Money Systems
Our Insular Possessions
Growth of Population
Trusts
Banks and Banking
Immigration
Capital and Labor
Education
Inventions
Suffrage
Centralization of Government
Strikes and Lockouts
Panics and Business Depressions
Commerce
Taxation
Manufacturing
Labor Unions
Foreign Commerce
Agriculture
Postal Service
Army
Government Control of Corporations
Municipal Government
Navy
Factory Labor

Wages
Courts of Law
Charities
Crime
Fire Protection
Roads and Road Transportation
Newspapers and Magazines
National Defense
Conservation of Natural Resources
Liquor Problems
Parks and Playgrounds
Housing Conditions
Mining
Health, Sanitation, etc.
Pensions
Unemployment
Child Labor
Women in Industry
Cost of Living
Pure Food Control
Savings Banks
Water Supply of Cities
Prisons
Recreations and Amusements
Co-operative Buying and Selling
Insurance
Hospitals

After drawing up such lists of topics for study, they should be assigned to grammar grades and high school according to the degree of maturity necessary for their comprehension. Naturally as much as possible should be covered in the grammar grades. Such as cannot be covered there should be covered as early as practicable in the high school, since so large a number of students drop out, and all need the work. Of course, this would involve a radical revision of the high school courses in history. It is not here recommended that any such changes be attempted abruptly. There are too many other conditions that require readjustment at the same time. It must all be a gradual growth.

Naturally, students must have some familiarity with the general time relations of history and the general chronological movements of affairs before they can understand the more or less specialized treatment of individual topics. Preliminary studies are therefore both necessary and desirable in the intermediate and grammar grades for the purpose of giving the general background. During these grades a great wealth of historical materials should be stored up. Pupils should acquire much familiarity with the history of the ancient oriental nations, Judea, Greece, Rome, the states of modern Europe and America. The purpose should be to give a general, and in the beginning a relatively superficial, overview of the world's history for the sake of perspective. The reading should be biographical, anecdotal, thrilling dramas of human achievement, rich with human interest. It should be at every stage of the work on the level with the understanding and degree of maturity of the pupils, so that much reading can be covered rapidly. Given the proper conditions—chiefly an abundance of the proper books supplied in sets large enough for classes—pupils can cover a large amount of ground, obtain a wealth of historical experience, and acquire a great quantity of useful information, the main outlines of which are remembered without much difficulty. They can in this manner lay a broad historical foundation for the study of the social topics that should begin by the seventh grade and continue throughout the high school.

The textbooks of the present type can be employed as a part of this preliminary training. Read in their entirety and read rapidly, they give one that perspective which comes from a comprehensive view of the entire field. But they are too brief, abstract, and barren to afford valuable concrete historical experience. They are excellent reference books for gaining and keeping historical perspective.

Reading of the character that we have here called preliminary should not cease as the other historical studies are taken up. The general studies should certainly continue for some portion of the time through the grammar grades and high school, but it probably should be mainly supervised reading of interesting materials rather than recitation and examination work.

We would recommend that the high schools give careful attention to the recommendation of the National Education Association Committee on the Reorganization of the Secondary Course of Study in History.

CIVICS

Civic training scarcely finds a place upon the elementary school program. The manual suggests that one-quarter of the history time—10 to 20 minutes per week—in the fifth and sixth grades should be given to a discussion of such civic topics as the department of public service, street cleaning, garbage disposal, health and sanitation, the city water supply, the mayor and the council, the treasurer, and the auditor. The topics are important, but the time allowed is inadequate and the pupils of these grades are so immature that no final treatment of such complicated matters is possible. For seventh and eighth grades, the manual makes no reference to civics. This is the more surprising because Cleveland is a city in which there has been no end of civic discussion and progressive human-welfare effort. The extraordinary value of civic education in the elementary school, as a means of furthering civic welfare, should have received more decided recognition.

The elementary teachers and principals of Cleveland might profitably make such a civic survey as that made in Cincinnati as the method of discovering the topics that should enter into a grammar grade course. The heavy emphasis upon this subject should be reserved for the later grades of the elementary school.

In the high schools, a little is being accomplished. In the academic high schools, those who take the classical course receive no civics whatever. It is not even elective for them. Those who take the scientific or English courses may take civics as a half-year elective. In the technical high schools it is required of all for a half-year. The course is offered only in the senior year, except in the High School of Commerce, where it is offered in the third. As a result of these various circumstances, the majority of students who enter and complete the course in the high schools of Cleveland receive no civic training whatever—not even the inadequate half-year of work that is available for a few.

Whether the deficiencies here pointed out are serious or not depends in large measure upon the character of the other social subjects, such as history and geography. If these are developed in full and concrete ways, they illumine large numbers of our difficult social problems. It is probable that the larger part of the informational portions of civic training should be imparted through these other social subjects. Whether very much of this is actually done at present is doubtful; for the history teaching, as has already been noted, is much underdeveloped, and while somewhat further advanced, geography work is still far from adequate at the time this report is written.

GEOGRAPHY

Geography in Cleveland is given the customary amount of time, though it is distributed over the grades in a somewhat unusual way. It is exceptionally heavy in the intermediate grades and correspondingly light in the grammar grades. As geography, like all other subjects, is more and more humanized and socialized in its reference, much more time will be called for in the last two grammar grades.

TABLE 9.—-TIME GIVEN TO GEOGRAPHY

Grade	Hours per year		Per cent of grade time	
	Cleveland	50 cities	Cleveland	50 cities
1	0	16	0.0	1.8
2	0	7	0.0	0.8
3	28	50	3.2	5.4
4	101	83	11.4	8.5
5	125	102	14.3	11.2
6	125	107	14.3	11.0
7	57	98	6.4	9.9
8	57	76	6.4	7.6
Total	493	539	7.2	7.1

As laid out in the manual now superseded, and as observed in the regular classrooms, the work has been forbiddingly formal. In the main it has consisted of the teacher assigning to the pupils a certain number of paragraphs or pages in the textbook as the next lesson, and then questioning them next day to ascertain how much of this printed material they have remembered and how well. It has not consisted of stimulating and guiding the children toward intelligent inquisitiveness and inquiring interest as to the world, and the skies above, and waters round about, and the conditions of nature that limit and shape the development of mankind.

That the latter is the proper end of geographical teaching is being recognized in developing the new course of study in this subject. Industries, commerce, agriculture, and modes of living are becoming the centers about which geographic thought and experience are gathered. The best work now being done here is thoroughly modern. Unfortunately it is not yet great in amount in even the best of the schools, still less in the majority. But the direction of progress is unmistakable and unquestionably correct.

As in the reading, so in geography, right development of the course of study must depend in large measure upon the material equipment that is at the same time provided. It sounds like a legitimate evasion to say that education is a spiritual process, and that good teachers and willing, obedient, and industrious pupils are about all that is required. As a matter of fact, just as modern business has found it necessary to install one-hundred-dollar typewriters to take the place of the penny quill pens, so must education, to be efficient, develop and employ the elaborate tools needed by new and complex modern conditions, and set aside the tools that were adequate in a simpler age. The proper teaching of geography requires an abundance of reading materials of the type that will permit pupils to enter vividly into the varied experience of all classes of people in all parts of the world. In the supplementary books now furnished the schools, only a beginning has been made. The schools need 10 times as much geographical reading as that now found in the best equipped school.

It would be well to drop the term "supplementary." This reading should be the basic geographic experience, the fundamental instrument of the teaching. All else is supplementary. The textbook then becomes a reference book of maps, charts, summaries, and a treatment for the sake of perspective. Maps, globes, pictures, stereoscopes, stereopticon, moving-picture machine, models, diagrams, and museum materials, are all for the purpose of developing ideas and imagery of details. The reading should become and remain fundamental and central. The quantity required is so great as to make it necessary for the city to furnish the books. While the various other things enumerated are necessary for complete effectiveness, many of them could well wait until the reading materials are sufficiently supplied.

In the high schools the clear tendency is to introduce more of the industrial and commercial geography and to diminish the time given to the less valuable physiography. The development is not yet vigorous. The high school geography departments, so far as observed, have not yet altogether attained the social point of view. But they are moving in that direction. On the one hand, they now need stimulation; and on the other, to be supplied with the more advanced kinds of such material equipment as already suggested for the elementary schools.

DRAWING AND APPLIED ART

The elementary schools are giving the usual proportion of time to drawing and applied art. The time is distributed, however, in a somewhat unusual, but probably justifiable, manner. Whereas the subject usually receives more time in the primary grades than in the grammar grades, in Cleveland, in quite the reverse way, the subject receives its greatest emphasis in the higher grades.

TABLE 10. — TIME GIVEN TO DRAWING

Grade	Hours per year		Per cent of grade time	
	Cleveland	50 cities	Cleveland	50 cities
1	47	98	6.5	11.3
2	47	54	5.3	6.0
3	47	56	5.3	6.2
4	47	53	5.3	5.5
5	57	50	6.4	5.2
6	57	50	6.4	5.1
7	57	50	6.4	5.0
8	57	49	6.4	4.9
Total	416	460	6.1	6.1

Drawing has been taught in Cleveland as a regular portion of the curriculum since 1849. It has therefore had time for substantial growth; and it appears to have been successful. Recent developments in the main have been wholesome and in line with best modern progress. The course throughout attempts to develop an understanding and appreciation of the principles of graphic art plus ability to use these principles through practical application in constructive activities of an endlessly varied sort.

Occasionally the work appears falsetto and even sentimental. It is often applied in artificial schoolroom ways to things without significance. General grade teachers cannot be specialists in the multiplicity of things demanded of them; it is not therefore surprising that they sometimes lack skill, insight, ingenuity, and resourcefulness. Too often the teachers do not realize that the study of drawing and design is for the serious purpose of giving to pupils a language and form of thought of the greatest practical significance in our present age. The result is a not infrequent use of schoolroom exercises that do not greatly aid the pupils as they enter the busy world of practical affairs.

These shortcomings indicate incompleteness in the development. Where the teaching is at its best in both the elementary and high schools of Cleveland, the work exhibits balanced understanding and complete modernness. The thing needed is further expansion of the best, and the extension of this type of work through specially trained departmental teachers to all parts of the city.

There should be a larger amount of active co-operation between the teachers of art and design and the teachers of manual training; also between both sets of teachers and the general community.

MANUAL TRAINING AND HOUSEHOLD ARTS

In the grammar grades manual and household training receives an average proportion of the time. In the grades before the seventh, the subject receives considerably less than the usual amount of time.

TABLE 11. — TIME GIVEN TO MANUAL TRAINING

Grade	Hours per year		Per cent of grade time	
	Cleveland	50 cities	Cleveland	50 cities
1	32	42	4.3	4.8
2	32	47	3.5	5.1
3	32	40	3.5	4.5
4	32	45	3.5	4.6
5	38	50	4.3	5.2
6	38	57	4.3	5.8
7	63	72	7.1	7.1
8	63	74	7.1	7.4
Total	330	427	4.8	5.6

It is easy to see the social and educational justification of courses in sewing, cooking, household sanitation, household decoration, etc., for the girls. They assist in the training for complicated vocational activities performed in some degree at least by most women. Where women are so situated that they do not actually perform them, they need, for properly supervising others and for making intelligible and appreciative use of the labors of others, a considerable understanding of these various matters.

Where this work for girls is at its best in Cleveland, it appears to be of a superior character. Those who are in charge of the best are in a position to advise as to further extensions and developments. It is not difficult to discern certain of these. It would appear, for example, that sewing should find some place at least in the work of seventh and eighth grades. The girl who does not go on to high school is greatly in need of more advanced training in sewing than can be given in the sixth grade. Each building having a household arts room should possess a sewing machine or two, at the very least. The academic high schools are now planning to offer courses in domestic science. As in the technical high schools, all of this work should involve as large a degree of normal responsibility as possible.

We omit discussion here of the specialized vocational training of women, since this is handled in other reports of the Survey.

When we turn to the manual training of the boys, we are confronted with problems of much greater difficulty. Women's household occupations, so far as retained in the home, are unspecialized. Each well-trained household worker does or supervises much the same range of things as every other. To give the entire range of household occupations to all girls is a simple and logical arrangement.

But man's labor is greatly specialized throughout. There is no large remnant of unspecialized labor common to all, as in the case of women. To all girls we give simply this unspecialized remnant, since it is large and important. But in the case of men the unspecialized field has disappeared. There is nothing of labor to give to boys except that which has become specialized.

A fundamental problem arises. Shall we give boys access to a variety of specialized occupations so that they may become acquainted, through responsible performance, with the wide and diversified field of man's labor? Or shall we give them some less specialized sample out of that diversified field so that they may obtain, through contact and experience, some knowledge of the things that make up the world of productive labor?

Cleveland's reply, to judge from actual practices, is that a single sample will be sufficient for all except those who attend technical and special schools. The city has therefore chosen joinery and cabinet-making as this sample. In the fifth and sixth grades work begins in simple knife-work for an hour a week under the direction of women teachers. In the seventh and eighth grades it becomes benchwork for an hour and a half per week, and is taught by a special manual training teacher, always a man. In the academic high schools the courses in joinery and cabinet-making bring the pupils to greater proficiency, but do not greatly extend the course in width.

Much of this work is of a rather formal character, apparently looking toward that manual discipline formerly called "training of eye and hand," instead of consciously answering to the demands of social purposes. The regular teachers look upon the fifth and sixth grade sloyd[*sic] which they teach with no great enthusiasm. Seventh and eighth grade teachers do not greatly value the work.

The household arts courses for the girls have social purposes in view. As a result they are kept vitalized, and are growing increasingly vital in the work of the city. Is it not possible also to vitalize the manual training of the boys—unspecialized pre-vocational training, we ought to call it—by giving it social purpose?

The principal of one of the academic high schools emphasized in conversation the value of manual training for vocational guidance—a social purpose. It permitted boys, he said, to try themselves out and to find their vocational tastes and aptitudes. The purpose is undoubtedly a valid one. The limitation of the method is that joinery and cabinet-making cannot help a boy to try himself out for metal work, printing, gardening, tailoring, or commercial work.

If vocational guidance is to be a controlling social purpose, the manual training work will have to be made more diversified so that one can try out his tastes and abilities in a number of lines. And, moreover, each kind of work must be kept as much like responsible work out in the world as possible. In keeping work normal, the main thing is that the pupils bear actual responsibility for the doing of actual work. This is rather difficult to arrange; but it is necessary before the activities can be lifted above the level of the usual manual training shop. The earliest stages of the training will naturally be upon what is little more than a play level. It is well for schools to give free rein to the constructive instinct and to provide the fullest and widest possible opportunities for its exercise. But if boys are to try out their aptitudes for work and their ability to bear responsibility in work, then they must try themselves out on the work level.

Let the manual training actually look toward vocational guidance; the social purpose involved will vitalize the work.

There is a still more comprehensive social purpose which the city should consider. Owing to the interdependence of human affairs, men need to be broadly informed as to the great world of productive labor. Most of our civic and social problems are at bottom industrial problems. Just as we use industrial history and industrial geography as means of giving youth a wide vision of the fields of man's work, so must we also use actual practical activities as means of making him familiar in a concrete way with materials and processes in their details, with the nature of work, and with the nature of responsibility. On the play level, therefore, constructive activities should be richly diversified. This diversity of opportunity should continue to the work level. One cannot really know the nature of work or of work responsibility except as it is learned through experience. Let the manual training adopt the social purpose here mentioned, provide the opportunities, means, and processes that it demands, and the work will be wondrously vitalized.

It is well to mention that the program suggested is a complicated one on the side of its theory and a difficult one on the side of its practice. In the planning it is well to look to the whole program. In the work itself it is well to remember that one step at a time, and that secure, is a good way to avoid stumbling.

Printing and gardening are two things that might well be added to the manual training program. Both are already in the schools in some degree. They might well be considered as desirable portions of the manual training of all. They lend themselves rather easily to responsible performance on the work level. There are innumerable things that a school can print for use in its work. In so doing, pupils can be given something other than play. Also in the home gardening, supervised for educational purposes, it is possible to introduce normal work-motives. By the time the city has developed these two things it will have at the same time developed the insight necessary for attacking more difficult problems.

ELEMENTARY SCIENCE

This subject finds no place upon the program. No elaborate argument should be required to convince the authorities in charge of the school system of a modern city like Cleveland that in this ultrascientific age the children who do not go beyond the elementary school—and they constitute a majority—need to possess a working knowledge of the rudiments of science if they are to make their lives effective.

The future citizens of Cleveland need to know something about electricity, heat, expansion and contraction of gases and solids, the mechanics of machines, distillation, common chemical reactions and a host of other things about science that are bound to come up in the day's work in their various activities.

Considered from the practical standpoint of actual human needs, the present almost complete neglect of elementary science is indefensible. The minute amount of such teaching now introduced in the language lessons for composition purposes is so small as to be almost negligible. The topics are not chosen for their bearing upon human needs. There is no laboratory work.

Naturally much of the elementary science to be taught should be introduced in connection with practical situations in kitchen, school garden, shop, sanitation, etc. Certainly the applied science should be as full as possible. But preliminary to this there ought to be systematic presentation of the elements of various sciences in rapid ways for overview and perspective.

To try to teach the elements only "incidentally" as they are applied is to fail to see them in their relations, and therefore to fail in understanding them. Intensive studies by way of filling in the details may well be in part incidental. But systematic superficial introductory work is needed by way of giving pupils their bearings in the various fields of science. The term "superficial" is used advisedly. There is an introductory stage in the teaching of every such subject when the work should be superficial and extensive. This stage paves the way for depth and intensity, which must be reached before education is accomplished.

HIGH SCHOOL SCIENCE

Having no elementary science in the grades, one naturally expects to find in the high school a good introductory course in general science, similar in organization to that suggested for the elementary stage. But nowhere is there anything that even remotely suggests such a course. Students who take the classical course get their first glimpse of modern science in the third or fourth high school year, when they have an opportunity to elect a course in physics or chemistry of the usual traditional stamp. No opportunity is given them for so much as a glimpse of the world's biological background. Those who take the scientific or English course have access to physical geography and to an anemic biological course entitled, "Physiology and Botany," which few take. Students of the High School of Commerce have their first contacts with modern science in a required course in chemistry in the third year, and elective physics in the fourth year. In the technical high schools the first science for the boys is systematic chemistry in the second year and physics in the third. They have no opportunity of contact with any biological science. The girls have "botany and physiology" in their first year.

The city needs to organize preliminary work in general science for the purpose of paving the way to the more intensive science work of the later years. A portion of this should be found in the elementary school and taught by departmental science teachers; and a portion in the first year of the high school. As junior high schools are developed, most of this work should be included in their courses.

As to the later organization of the work, the two technical high schools clearly indicate the modern trend of relating the science teaching to practical labors. What is needed is a wider expansion of this phase of the work without losing sight of the need at the same time for a systematic and general teaching of the sciences. It is a difficult task to make the science teaching vital and modern for the academic high schools, since they have so few contacts with the practical labors of the world. Cleveland needs to see its schools more as a part of the world of affairs, and not so much as a hot-house nursery isolated from the world and its vital interests.

PHYSIOLOGY AND HYGIENE

Teaching in matters pertaining to health is given but a meagre amount of time in the elementary schools. While the school program shows one 15-minute period each week in the first four grades, and one 30-minute period each week in the four upper grades, it appears that in actual practice the subject receives even less time than this. In the attempt to observe the class work in physiology and hygiene, a member of the Survey staff went on one day to four different classrooms at the hour scheduled on the program. In two cases the time was given over to grammar, in one to arithmetic, and in one to music. This represents practice that is not unusual. The subject gets pushed off the program by one of the so-called "essentials." It is difficult to see why health-training is not an essential. In a letter to the School Board, February 8, 1915, Superintendent Frederick wrote:

"The teaching of physiology and hygiene should become a matter of serious moment in our course of study. At present it is not systematically presented in the elementary schools: and in the high schools it is an elective study only in the senior year. My judgment is that it should become a definite part of the program, as a required study in the seventh and eighth grades."

The small nominal amount of time as compared with the time usually expended is partially shown in Table 12. Professor Holmes' figures for the 50 cities include elementary science along with the physiology and hygiene.

TABLE 12. — TIME GIVEN TO SCIENCE, PHYSIOLOGY, HYGIENE

	Hours per year		Per cent of grade time	
Grade	Cleveland	50 cities	Cleveland	50 cities

1 | 10 | 37 | 1.3 | 4.3
2 | 10 | 41 | 1.1 | 4.5
3 | 10 | 40 | 1.1 | 4.4
4 | 10 | 37 | 1.1 | 3.8
5 | 19 | 34 | 2.1 | 3.5
6 | 19 | 40 | 2.1 | 4.2
7 | 19 | 45 | 2.1 | 4.5
8 | 19 | 57 | 2.1 | 5.7
– – –+– – – – – –+– – – – – –+– – – – – –+– – – – – –
Total | 116 | 331 | 1.7 | 4.4
– – –+– – – – – –+– – – – – –+– – – – – –+– – – – – –

In addition to the work of the regular teachers in this subject, a certain amount of instruction is given by the school physicians and nurses. In his report to the Board, 1913, Dr. Peterson writes:

"Health instruction is given by doctors and nurses in personal talks to pupils, talks to whole schools, tooth-brush drills conducted in many schools, and in visits into the homes by the nurses. Conscious effort is continually made by all doctors and nurses to inspire to right living all of the children with whom they come in contact."

Looking somewhat to the future, it can be affirmed that the school physicians and nurses are the ones who ought to give the teaching in this subject. After giving the preliminary ideas in the classrooms, they alone are in position to follow up the various matters and see that the ideas are assimilated through being put into practice both at school and at home. At present, however, 16 physicians and 27 nurses have 75,000 children to inspect, of whom more than half have defects that require following up. It is a physical impossibility for them to do much teaching until the force of school nurses is greatly increased.

For the present certain things may well be done:

1. A course in hygiene and sanitation, based upon an abundance of reading, should be drawn up and taught by the regular teachers in the grammar school grades. This course should be looked upon as merely preliminary to the more substantial portions of education in this field. The physicians and nurses should select the readings

and supervise the course to see that the materials are covered conscientiously and not slighted.

2. The schools should arrange for practical applications of the preparatory knowledge in as many ways as possible. Children in relays can look after the ventilation, temperature, humidity, dust, light, and other sanitary conditions of school-rooms and grounds. They can make sanitary surveys of their home district; engage in anti-fly, anti-mosquito, anti-dirt, and other campaigns; and report—for credit possibly—practical sanitary and hygienic activities carried on outside of school. Only as knowledge is put to work is it assimilated and the prime purpose of education accomplished.

3. The corps of school nurses should be gradually enlarged, and after a time they can be given any needed training for teaching that will enable them, as the work is departmentalized in the grammar grades, to become departmental teachers in this subject for a portion of their time. Their "follow-up" work will always give them their chief educational opportunity; but to prepare for this the classwork must give some systematized preparatory ideas.

In the high schools, training of boys in hygiene and sanitation is little developed. The only thing offered them is an elective half-year course in physiology in the senior year of the scientific and English courses in the academic high schools. In the classical course, and in the technical and commercial schools, they have not even this. Physiology is required of girls in the technical schools, and is elective in all but the classical course in the others. While in one or two of the high schools there is training in actual hygiene and sanitation, in most cases it is physiology and anatomy of a superficial preliminary type which is not put to use and which therefore mostly fails of normal assimilation.

The things recommended for the elementary schools need to be carried out in the high schools also.

PHYSICAL TRAINING

The city gives slightly more than the usual amount of time to physical training in the elementary schools. Except for first and second grades, where a slightly larger amount is set aside for the purpose, pupils are expected to receive one hour per week.

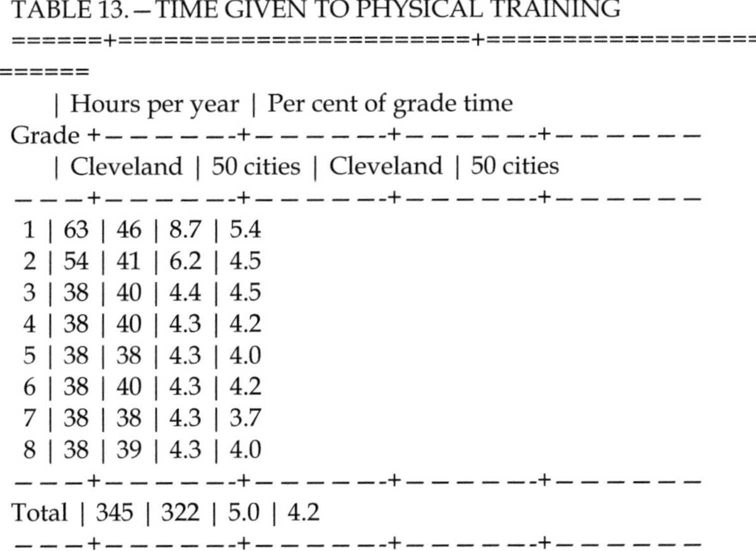

TABLE 13. — TIME GIVEN TO PHYSICAL TRAINING

Grade	Hours per year		Per cent of grade time	
	Cleveland	50 cities	Cleveland	50 cities
1	63	46	8.7	5.4
2	54	41	6.2	4.5
3	38	40	4.4	4.5
4	38	40	4.3	4.2
5	38	38	4.3	4.0
6	38	40	4.3	4.2
7	38	38	4.3	3.7
8	38	39	4.3	4.0
Total	345	322	5.0	4.2

Even though it is a little above the average amount of time, it is nevertheless too little. A week consists of 168 hours. After deducting 12 hours a day for sleep, meals, etc., there remain 84 hours per week to be used. In a state of nature this was largely used for physical play. Under the artificial conditions of modern city life, the nature of children is not changed. They still need huge amounts of active physical play for wholesome development. Most of this they will get away from the school, but as urban conditions take away proper play opportunities, the loss in large degree has to be made good by systematic community effort in establishing and maintaining playgrounds and playrooms for 12 months in the year. The school and its immediate environment is the logical place for this development.

The course of study lays out a series of obsolescent Swedish gymnastics for each of the years. The work observed was mechanical, perfunctory, and lacking in vitality. Sandwiched in between exhausting intellectual drill, it has the value of giving a little relief and rest. This is good, but it is not sufficiently positive to be called physical training.

Very desirable improvements in the course are being advocated by the directors and supervisors of the work. They are recommending, and introducing where conditions will permit, the use of games, athletics, folk dances, etc. The movements should be promoted by the city in every possible way. At present the regular teachers as a rule have not the necessary point of view and do not sufficiently value the work. Special teachers and play leaders need to be employed. Material facilities should be extended and improved. Some of the school grounds are too small; the surfacing is not always well adapted to play; often apparatus is not supplied; indoor playrooms are insufficient in number, etc. These various things need to be supplied before the physical training curriculum can be modernized.

In the high schools two periods of physical training per week in academic and commercial schools, and three or four periods per week in the technical schools, are prescribed for the first two years of the course. In the last two years it is omitted from the program in all but the High School of Commerce, where it is optional. With one or two exceptions, the little given is mainly indoor gymnastics of a formal sort owing to the general lack of sufficiently large athletic fields, tennis courts, baseball diamonds, and other necessary facilities.

Special commendation must be accorded the home-room basis of organizing the athletics of the technical high schools. Probably no plan anywhere employed comes nearer to reaching the entire student body in a vital way.

With the exceptions referred to, it seems that the city has not sufficiently considered the indispensable need of huge amounts of physical play on the part of adolescents as the basis of full and lifelong physical vitality. High school students represent the best youth of the community. Their efficiency is certainly the greatest single asset of the new generation. There are scores of other expensive things that the city can better afford to neglect. The one thing it can least afford to sacrifice on the altar of economy is the vitality of its citizens of tomorrow.

MUSIC

In the elementary schools Cleveland is giving considerably more than the average amount of time to music. In the high schools, except for a one-hour optional course in the High School of Commerce, the subject is developed only incidentally and given no credit. It is entirely pertinent to inquire why music should be so important for the grammar school age and then lose all of this importance as soon as the high school is reached.

TABLE 14. — TIME GIVEN TO MUSIC

Grade	Hours per year		Per cent of grade time	
	Cleveland	50 cities	Cleveland	50 cities
1	47	45	6.5	5.2
2	54	48	6.1	5.3
3	54	47	6.1	5.1
4	54	48	6.1	4.9
5	51	45	5.7	4.7
6	51	45	5.7	4.6
7	51	45	5.7	4.4
8	51	44	5.7	4.4
Total	413	367	6.0	4.8

The probability is either that it is over-valued for the elementary school and should receive diminished time; or it is under-valued for the high school and should be given the dignity and the consideration of a credit course, as it is in many progressive high schools. It cannot be urged that the subject is finished in the elementary schools. Pupils in fact receive only an introductory training in vocal music. The whole field of instrumental music remains untouched. It seems the city ought to consider the question of whether the course ought not to be much expanded and continued throughout the high school period as an elective subject. However, in considering the question it should be kept in mind that there are very many things of more importance and of far more pressing immediate necessity.

FOREIGN LANGUAGES

German has long been taught in the elementary schools. Until less than 10 years ago it was taught in all grades beginning with the first. More recently it has been confined to the four upper grades. Beginning with the present year, it is taught only in the seventh and eighth grades. The situation is so well presented in the report of the Educational Commission of 1906 that further discussion here is unnecessary. They summarize their discussion of the teaching of German in the elementary schools as follows:

"Such teaching originated in a nationalistic feeling and demand on the part of German immigrants, and not in any educational or pedagogical necessity.

"It aimed to induce the children of Germans to attend the public schools, where they would learn English and be sooner Americanized.

"For 15 years [now 25 years] past, German immigration has almost ceased, and other European nationalities, as the Bohemians, Poles, and Italians, have taken their place numerically.

"The children of the earlier German immigrants are already Americanized and use the English language freely, and those later born, of the second and third generations, no longer need to be taught
German in the schools beginning at six years of age.

"It is demonstrated by experience and by abundant testimony that children neither from German nor from English-speaking families really learn much German in the primary and grammar grades, that is, from six to 13 years of age.

"Hence the Commission recommends that the teaching of German in these grades be discontinued and that the German language be taught only in the high schools.

"It is admitted that those who begin German in the high school, after the second year, can keep up with and do as good work in the same classes as those who have had eight years of German in the primary and grammar grades and two years in the high schools."

The form of argument that once was valid for including German in the elementary course of study may now be valid for Polish, Hungarian, Bohemian and Italian, for the children of the first generation of these nationalities. Properly done, it is a means of preventing the children's drifting from the parental moorings. After the first generation, it would not be needed.

It is impossible, in the limited space at our disposal, to discuss comprehensively so complicated a topic as foreign languages in the high school. One group of educators sturdily defends the traditional classical course, with its great emphasis on Greek and Latin, while another group as urgently insists that if any foreign languages are taught, they must be the modern ones. These opposing schools of thought are profoundly sincere in their conflicting beliefs. Each side is absolutely certain that it is right and is unalterably of the opinion that there is no other side of the question to be even so much as considered. Anything that agrees with its own side is based on reason; anything opposed is but ignorant prejudice. Under the circumstances the disinterested outsider may well suspect that where there is so much sincerity and conviction, there must be much truth on both sides. And undoubtedly this is the case.

Latin is a living language in our country in that it provides half of our vocabulary. Pupils who would know English well should have a good knowledge of this living Latin. If the Latinists would shift their ground to this living Latin and provide means of teaching it fully and effectively for modern purposes, it is possible that the opposing schools of thought might here find common ground upon which all could stand with some degree of comfort and toleration. When Latin study of the character here suggested is devised, it ought to be opened up to the students of all courses as an elective, so that it could be taken by all who wish a full appreciation and understanding of their semi-Latin mother tongue. Such a study ought to be required of the clerical students of the High School of

Commerce. In the meantime, however, all will have to wait until the Latinists have provided the plans and the materials.

In the new so-called English course in the academic high schools required foreign languages are omitted entirely. In the third and fourth years German or Spanish is made elective. This gives rise to several questions. If the foreign language is studied simply as preparation for the leisure occupation of reading its literature — the only value of the course in the case of most who take it — why should not French be elective also? By far the largest of the world's literatures, outside of the English, is the French. The Spanish has but a small literature; and while Germany has excelled in many things, belles-lettres is not one of them. Another question relates to the placing of these electives. If one is to study a foreign language at all, it is usually thought best to begin earlier than the third year of the high school, so as to finish these simple matters that can be done by children and gain time in the later years for the more complicated matters that require mature judgment.

DIFFERENTIATION OF COURSES

Courses of training based upon human needs should be diversified where conditions are diversified. Uniform courses of study for all schools within a city were justifiable in a former simpler age, when the schools were caring only for needs that were common to all classes. But as needs have differentiated in our large industrial cities, courses of training must also become differentiated. In Cleveland this principle has been recognized in organizing the work of the special schools and classes. For all the regular elementary schools, however, a uniform course of study has been used. Under the present administration, principals and teachers are nominally permitted wide latitude in its administration.

A large part of this freedom is taken away by two things. One is the use by the city of the plan of leaving textbooks to private purchase. For perfectly obvious reasons, so long as textbooks are privately purchased, a uniform series of textbooks must be definitely prescribed for the entire city. Uniform textbooks do not necessarily enforce a uniform curriculum. In usual practice, however, they do enforce it as completely as a prescribed uniform course of study manual. As the schools of different sections of the city are allowed to experiment and to develop variations from the course of study, they should be allowed greater freedom in choosing the textbooks that will best serve in teaching their courses.

The second condition enforcing a uniform course of study in certain subjects is the use of uniform examinations in those subjects. We would merely suggest here that it is possible to use supervisory examinations without making them uniform for all schools. Different types of school may well have different types of examination.

Different social classes often exist within the same school. Administrative limitations probably must prevent the use of more than one course of study in a single elementary school. But as the work of the grammar grades is departmentalized, and as junior high schools are developed, it will become possible to offer alternative courses in these grades. Those practically certain of going on to higher educational work requiring foreign languages and higher mathematics should probably be permitted to begin these studies by the sixth or seventh grade. On the other hand, those who are practically certain to drop out of school at the end of the grammar grades or junior high school should have full opportunities for applied science, applied design, practical mathematics, civics, hygiene, vocational studies, etc. When the necessary studies are once organized and departmental work introduced, it is not difficult to arrange for the necessary differentiation of courses in the same school.

Finally, courses of study should provide for children of differing natural ability. Extra materials and opportunities should be provided for children of large capacity; and abbreviated courses for those of less than normal ability. In departmentalized grammar grades and junior high schools this can be taken care of rather easily by permitting the brighter pupils to carry more studies than normal, and the backward ones a smaller number than normal. Under the present elementary school organization with classes so large and with so many things for the teachers to do, it is practically impossible to effect such desirable differentiations.

SUMMARY

1. The fundamental social point of view of this discussion of the courses of study of the Cleveland schools is that effective teaching is preparation for adult life through participation in the activities of life.

2. The schools of Cleveland devote far more time to reading than do those of the average city. In too large measure this time is employed in mastering the mechanics of reading and in the analytical study of the manner in which the words are combined in sentences and the sentences in paragraphs. The main object of the reading should be the mastery of the thought rather than the study of the construction. Through it the children should gain life-long habits of exploring, through reading, the great fields of history, industry, applied science, life in other lands, travel, invention, biography, and wholesome fiction. To this end the work should be made more extensive and less intensive. As an indispensable means toward this end the books should be supplied by the schools instead of being purchased by the parents.

3. The teaching of spelling should aim to give the pupils complete mastery over those words which they need to use in writing and it should instil in them the permanent habit of watching their spelling as they write. Drill on lists of isolated words should give way to practice in spelling correctly every word in everything written. The dictionary habit should be cultivated, and every written lesson should be a spelling lesson.

4. The time devoted to language, composition, and grammar is about the same as in the average city. The chief result of the work as done in Cleveland is to enable the pupil to recite well on textbook grammar and to pass examinations in the subject. The work in technical grammar should be continued for the purpose of giving the pupils a foundation acquaintance with forms, terms, relations, and grammatical perspective, but this training need not be so extensive and intensive as at present. The time saved should be given to oral

and written expression in connection with the reading of history, geography, industrial studies, civics, sanitation, and the like. Facility and accuracy in oral and written expression are developed through practice rather than through precept. They are perfected through the conscious and unconscious imitation of good models rather than through the advanced study of technical grammar. Only as knowledge is put to work is it really learned or assimilated.

5. Cleveland gives more time to mathematics than does the average city. The content of courses in mathematics is to be determined by human needs. A fundamental need of our scientific age is more accurate quantitative thinking about our vocations, civic problems, taxation, income, insurance, expenditures, public improvements, and the multitude of other public and private problems involving quantities. We need to think accurately and easily in quantities, proportions, forms, and relationships. Arithmetic teaching, like the teaching of penmanship, is for the purpose of providing tools to be used in matters that lie beyond. The present course of study is of superior character, providing for efficient elementary training and dispensing with most of the things of little practical use. The greatest improvement in the work is to be found in its further carrying over into the other fields of school work and in applying it in other classes as well as in the arithmetic class. In the advanced classes mathematics should be differentiated according to the needs of different pupils. Algebra should be more closely related to practical matters and developed in connection with geometry and trigonometry.

6. History receives much less attention in this city than in the average city. The character of the work is really indicated by the last sentence of the eighth-grade history assignment: "The text of our book should be thoroughly mastered." The work is too brief, abstract, and barren to help the pupils toward an understanding of the social, political, economic, and industrial problems with which we are confronted. It should be amply supplemented by a wide range of reading on social welfare topics. This reading should be biographical, anecdotal, thrilling dramas of human achievement, rich with human interest. It should be at every stage on the level with the understanding and degree of maturity of the pupils so that much reading can be covered rapidly.

7. In Cleveland, where there has been an almost unequalled amount of civic discussion and progressive human-welfare effort, the teaching of civics in the public schools receives too little attention. It is recommended that the principals and teachers make such a civic survey as that made in Cincinnati as the method of discovering the topics that should enter into a grammar-grade course. Not much civics teaching should be attempted in the intermediate grades, but it should be given in the higher grades.

8. A new course of study in geography is now being put into use. The work as laid out in the old manual and as seen in the classrooms has been forbiddingly formal. It has mainly consisted of the teacher assigning to the pupils a certain number of paragraphs or pages in the textbook as the next lesson, and then questioning them next day to ascertain how much of this printed material they have remembered and how well. The new course of study recognizes, on the contrary, that the proper end of geographical teaching is rather to stimulate and guide the children toward an inquiring interest as to how the world is made, and the skies above, and the waters round about, and the conditions of nature that limit and determine in a measure the development of mankind. To attain this ideal will require in every school 10 times as adequate provision of geographical reading and geographical material as is now found in the best equipped school.

9. Drawing and applied art have been taught in Cleveland since 1849. The object of the teaching is to develop an understanding and appreciation of the principles of graphic art and ability to use these principles in practical applications. Where this work is done best, it shows, in both the elementary and high schools, balanced understanding and complete modernness. What is needed is extension of this best type of work to all parts of the city through specially trained departmental teachers.

10. Where teaching of household arts is at its best in Cleveland, it is of a superior character and should be extended along lines now being followed. Manual training for boys should be extended and broadened with a view to giving the pupils real contact with more types of industry than those represented by the present woodwork.

11. Elementary science finds no place in the course of study of Cleveland. The future citizens of Cleveland will need an understanding of electricity, heat, expansion and contraction of gases and solids, the mechanics of machines, distillations, common chemical reactions, and the multitude of other matters of science met with daily in their activities. The schools should help supply this need.

12. Teaching in matters pertaining to health is assigned little time in the elementary schools, and the time that is assigned to it is frequently given to something else. The subject gets pushed off the program by one of the so-called "essentials." A course in hygiene should be drawn up, and practical applications of the work should be arranged through having pupils look after the sanitary conditions of rooms and grounds. The school doctors and nurses should help in this teaching and practice.

13. Physical training is given about as much time as in the average city, but without adequate facilities for outdoor and indoor plays and games. At present the work is too largely of the formal gymnastic type. Desirable improvements in the course are being advocated by the directors and supervisors of the work. They are recommending and introducing, where conditions will permit, the use of games, athletics, folk dances, and the like. The movement should be promoted in every possible way.

14. In the elementary schools Cleveland gives more than the average amount of time to music, but in the high schools the subject is developed only incidentally and is given no credit. It is a question whether this arrangement is the right one, and in considering possible extensions it should be remembered that there are other subjects of far more pressing immediate necessity.

15. It is impossible in this brief report to discuss adequately so complicated a matter as that of the teaching of foreign languages in the high schools, but some of the most important of the questions at issue have been indicated as matters which the school authorities should continue to study until satisfactory solutions are reached.

16. Where school work in Cleveland is backward, it is because it has not yet taken on the social point of view. Where it is progressive, it is being developed on the basis of human needs. There is much of both kinds of work in Cleveland.

17. In a city with a population so diversified as is that of Cleveland, progress should be made steadily and consciously away from city-wide uniformity in courses of study and methods of teaching. There should be progressive differentiation of courses to meet the widely varying needs of the different sorts of children in different sections of the city.

CLEVELAND EDUCATION SURVEY REPORTS

These reports can be secured from the Survey Committee of the Cleveland Foundation, Cleveland, Ohio. They will be sent postpaid for 25 cents per volume with the exception of "Measuring the Work of the Public Schools" by Judd, "The Cleveland School Survey" by Ayres, and "Wage Earning and Education" by Lutz. These three volumes will be sent for 50 cents each. All of these reports may be secured at the same rates from the Division of Education of the Russell Sage Foundation, New York City.

Child Accounting in the Public Schools — Ayres.
Educational Extension — Perry.
Education through Recreation — Johnson.
Financing the Public Schools — Clark.
Health Work in the Public Schools — Ayres.
Household Arts and School Lunches — Boughton.
Measuring the Work of the Public Schools — Judd.
Overcrowded Schools and the Platoon Plan — Hartwell.
School Buildings and Equipment — Ayres.
Schools and Classes for Exceptional Children — Mitchell.
School Organization and Administration — Ayres.
The Public Library and the Public Schools — Ayres and McKinnie.
The School and the Immigrant — Miller.
The Teaching Staff — Jessup.
What the Schools Teach and Might Teach — Bobbitt.
The Cleveland School Survey (Summary) — Ayres.
* * * * *

Boys and Girls in Commercial Work — Stevens.
Department Store Occupations — O'Leary.
Dressmaking and Millinery — Bryner.
Railroad and Street Transportation — Fleming.
The Building Trades — Shaw.
The Garment Trades — Bryner.
The Metal Trades — Lutz.
The Printing Trades — Shaw.
Wage Earning and Education (Summary) — Lutz.